plus ONE

backstage {BE} exclusive

BY MARK SMEBY

Tommy nelson

DON'T MISS THE OTHER GREAT TITLES IN THE BACKSTAGE EXCLUSIVE SERIES—AVAILABLE NOW ON YOUR FAVORITE ARTISTS

Published in Nashville, Tennessee, by Tommy Nelson®, a division of Thomas Nelson, Inc.

Written by Mark Smeby
Cover design and logo by Lookout Design Group
Interior layout and design by Anderson-Thomas

For Backstage Exclusive – Thanks to Greg Lucid, Mitchell Solarek at Mitchell Management, the guys' families, Roy Roper, Dawn Verner and Joel Anderson at Anderson Thomas Design, Natalie Nichols Gillespie, Elise Joseph, Jennifer Consiglio, Neal Joseph, Laura Minchew, Robin Crouch, and the rest of the Tommy Nelson gang. Most importantly, huge thanks to Jeremy, Jason, Nate, Nathan, and Gabe—you're cooler than I dreamed.

PHOTO CREDITS Professional photos by James White. Other photography by Mark Smeby, Plus One and their families. Fan photos by Meagan Pramuk, Lynda Mueller, Kayleigh Cox, Stacia Tague, Ivy Moesner, Rachel and Sara Sharpton, Charlene Tow, Kristen Zavadil, Olivia Medlin, Natalie Shaver, Andria-Clair Bauerle and Amy Story.

Send your comments about this book to: plusone@tommynelson.com. Sorry—we can't promise a reply.

table of
contents

4   OVERVIEW OF THE BAND

8   MAKING THE PROMISE

12   TAKING IT TO THE WORLD

14   JASON PERRY

18   LIGHTS, CAMERA, ACTION!

20   JEREMY MHIRE

24   HIT THE ROAD

28   NATHAN WALTERS

32   IT'S NOT WHAT YOU MIGHT THINK

34   NATE COLE

38   HERE IN MY HEART

40   GABE COMBS

44   FACING THE FUTURE

46   FEAR NOT

47   TO THE FANS

48   JUST THE FACTS

plus
ONE

" We constantly hear testimonies and receive letters and e-mails from people who have been encouraged through our music. That is why we make the kind of music that we do. " – *Nate*

OVERVIEW OF
the band

PLUS ONE is not just another boy band. These five talented guys are committed to making a difference in the lives of everyone they come in contact with, whether on the radio or television, in concert, or in person.

NATE COLE, GABE COMBS, JEREMY MHIRE, JASON PERRY, AND NATHAN WALTERS are as close as brothers. This trait has been developed over the past couple of years, not only by living together in close quarters, but also through a common love of music and a shared desire to see their music impact the lives of people around the world.

"We constantly hear testimonies and receive letters and e-mails from people who have been encouraged through our music," Nate explained. "That is why we make the kind of music that we do."

MARCH 17, 2000 - Los Angeles

Tomorrow morning we're moving to Nashville. I'm excited – but at the same time i'm just starting to feel so at home here. I think LA has taught me a lot about people and even myself. Even in this town of stars and celebrities everyone still puts their pants on one leg at a time and at the end of the day the only difference is usually a few more zeros in their salary.

Jeremy

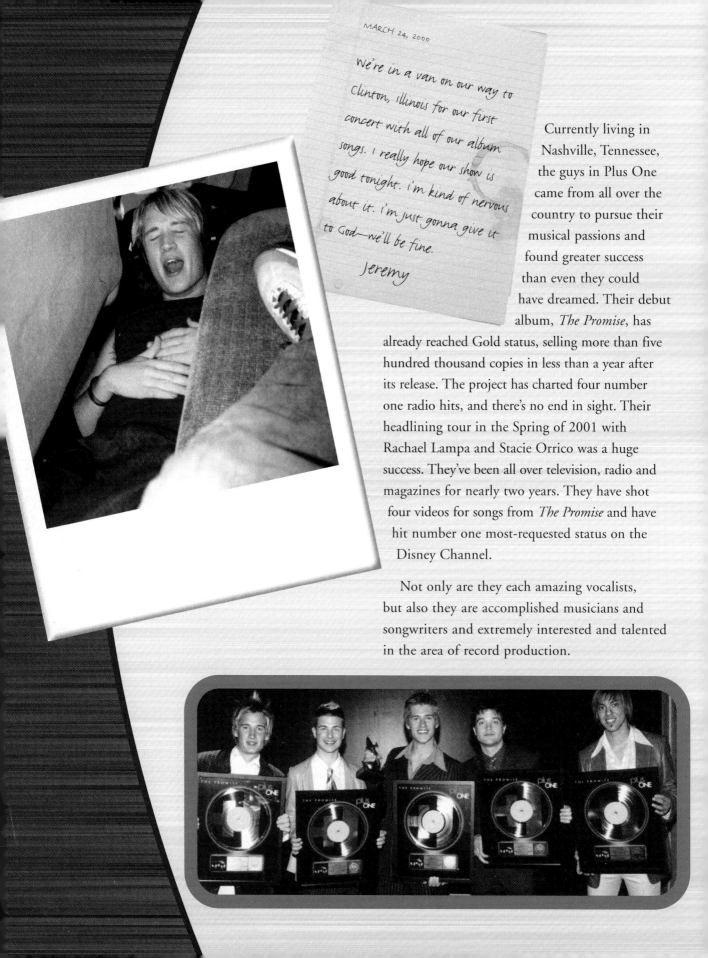

We're in a van on our way to Clinton, Illinois for our first concert with all of our album songs. I really hope our show is good tonight. I'm kind of nervous about it. I'm just gonna give it to God—we'll be fine.

Jeremy

Currently living in Nashville, Tennessee, the guys in Plus One came from all over the country to pursue their musical passions and found greater success than even they could have dreamed. Their debut album, *The Promise*, has already reached Gold status, selling more than five hundred thousand copies in less than a year after its release. The project has charted four number one radio hits, and there's no end in sight. Their headlining tour in the Spring of 2001 with Rachael Lampa and Stacie Orrico was a huge success. They've been all over television, radio and magazines for nearly two years. They have shot four videos for songs from *The Promise* and have hit number one most-requested status on the Disney Channel.

Not only are they each amazing vocalists, but also they are accomplished musicians and songwriters and extremely interested and talented in the area of record production.

APRIL 15, 2000—Nashville

Yesterday we had a dress rehearsal for about forty people from Atlantic Records. Every time we perform as a group I feel we're getting better, but there are still some rough edges.

Jeremy

Wherever this road of success takes them over the next few years, it is certain Plus One will be followed by millions of fans around the world.

People become fans of Plus One for many different reasons. But the reason they continue to be fans is because these five guys have hearts of gold. Plus One wants to reach the world, not so they can be huge stars, but so they will have the chance to reach more and more people with their encouraging message of hope.

"The underlying theme of the album would definitely be a message of hope: that God loves you and cares for you, and if you just put your trust and faith in Him, He'll never leave your side," Jason explained. "It's a very simple message. He's our 'plus one.' Wherever I go I know He's walking right alongside me (Hebrews 13:5)."

plus ONE

making
THE PROMISE

The making of *The Promise* was a whirlwind adventure. The first step was to find the right producers and songs. Together with people at 143 Records and their A&R person, Jaymes Foster-Levy, the band began listening to hundreds of song demos.

One of the most successful producers of all time (as well as the head of their label), David Foster, hosted a luncheon at Peer Music in Los Angeles. He invited all of the top songwriters and producers in L.A. Plus One performed two songs they had already found, including "The Promise." Fortunately, it was successful and

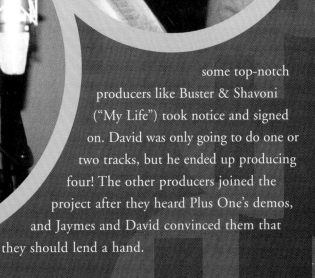

some top-notch producers like Buster & Shavoni ("My Life") took notice and signed on. David was only going to do one or two tracks, but he ended up producing four! The other producers joined the project after they heard Plus One's demos, and Jaymes and David convinced them that they should lend a hand.

Choosing the songs and producers happened at the same time. It was November, and they had to have a record done by March. They spent the next two months finishing song selections. Then when January rolled around, it was time to really get to work and start recording. Since there were twelve producers and several studios, the guys had a hard time remembering what city they were in many times. Literally every day was spent in a studio. By March, their label had to hire a driver to take them from one studio in the morning to another to finish a different song at night. It was a brutal time. Thankfully, God provided health because there could be no glitches if they were going to get it done.

The last song to be completed was "Last Flight Out". They recorded the song in Nashville. It was the only song they were able to record there.

On Being in the Studio:

GABE: You have to be patient in the studio. You have to do it so many times just to get your part right. Nathan has really good pitch, so he would finish quickly. So would Nate.

JASON: Sometimes I think I could've done better at very minute things, like the phrasing of certain words.

JEREMY: I strongly believe that the way the album and the group came together was in God's perfect will. From the producers to us, the songs, and the writers, everything was divinely appointed.

NATHAN: The best part was the food. Or playing Monopoly…

NATE: There is a lot of sitting around. When you're not singing, you have to be available. We watched movies and TV, worked on other songs, and mastered the PlayStation.

Taking it to the
WORLD

JEREMY: For three weeks we had the opportunity to visit the Philippines (which was special to me because of my family's heritage there), Thailand, Malaysia, and Singapore. It was a very busy trip with a crazy schedule, but it was awesome to see the results of our work when we left each country.

GABE: It was a crazy experience. It was so cool to go to the other side of the world and see people singing our songs. We would arrive at a city in Asia and have people screaming our names at the airport, giving us gifts of stuff we like just because we mentioned it in an interview or on our Web site.

JASON: It was crazy to find out that not only do we have fans in America, but also all over the world. We're called to go into all the world and preach the gospel, and I feel the message of Plus One is doing just that. I would love to go back, especially to Thailand and go to the beaches!

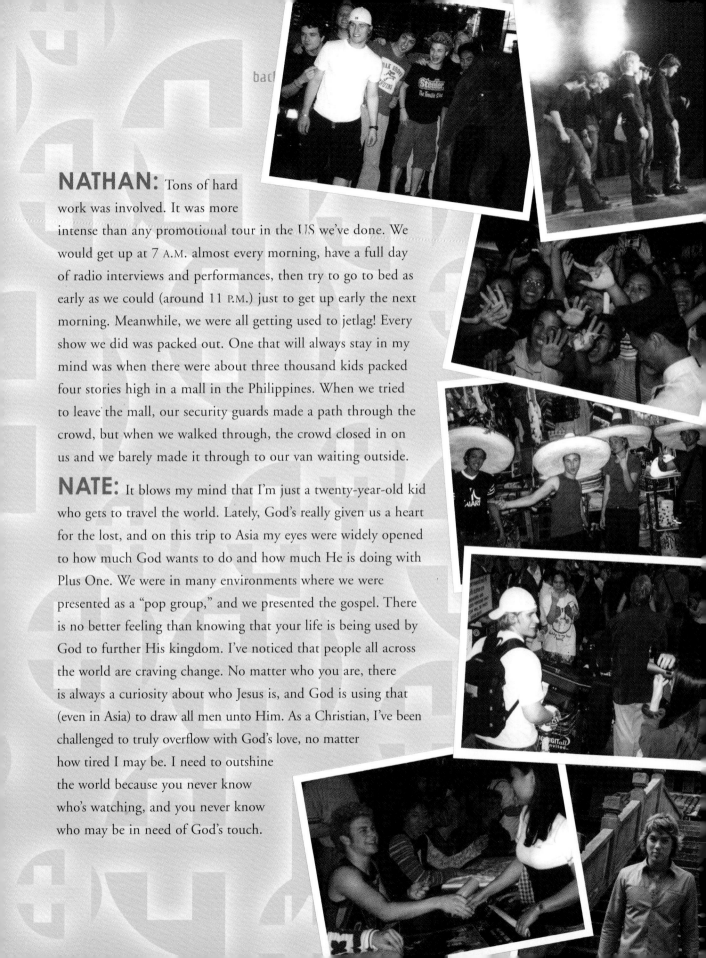

NATHAN: Tons of hard work was involved. It was more intense than any promotional tour in the US we've done. We would get up at 7 A.M. almost every morning, have a full day of radio interviews and performances, then try to go to bed as early as we could (around 11 P.M.) just to get up early the next morning. Meanwhile, we were all getting used to jetlag! Every show we did was packed out. One that will always stay in my mind was when there were about three thousand kids packed four stories high in a mall in the Philippines. When we tried to leave the mall, our security guards made a path through the crowd, but when we walked through, the crowd closed in on us and we barely made it through to our van waiting outside.

NATE: It blows my mind that I'm just a twenty-year-old kid who gets to travel the world. Lately, God's really given us a heart for the lost, and on this trip to Asia my eyes were widely opened to how much God wants to do and how much He is doing with Plus One. We were in many environments where we were presented as a "pop group," and we presented the gospel. There is no better feeling than knowing that your life is being used by God to further His kingdom. I've noticed that people all across the world are craving change. No matter who you are, there is always a curiosity about who Jesus is, and God is using that (even in Asia) to draw all men unto Him. As a Christian, I've been challenged to truly overflow with God's love, no matter how tired I may be. I need to outshine the world because you never know who's watching, and you never know who may be in need of God's touch.

Full Name: Jason Wayne Perry

Birthday: June 1, 1982

Nicknames: JuJu (from my mom), Jase, JP

Born in Ft. Thomas, KY — went to H.S. in Madison, IN

Jason is . . .

NATHAN: A good guy. He's changed a lot 'cause he's the youngest—from being really cocky, actually, to being more sensitive to how he comes across to people. He's into sports. He has a nice strong voice. He gives people time in order to show he cares.

GABE: Very confident—he knows what he wants and goes and gets it.

JEREMY: Musically, he's one of the very strong lead vocals. He sings with a lot of gospel influences. You believe him. He's got a really strong personality and qualities of a leader. He definitely has the ability to speak his mind and heart.

NATE: He's very passionate about what we're doing as a group and our mission.

HIMSELF: A man of God seeking after God's own heart. I'm a pretty enthusiastic type of person. I'm very driven; I like to take care of business.

Growing up:

My dad and my two brothers (one older and one younger) and I would go fishing out in the country. The road was so bumpy and hilly that we called it the bumpy road. It was so fun when we were really little. We were in church all the time. We ordered pizza every Sunday night after church and watched a movie. My dad and I were really close. We were always playing basketball or working out with my older brother. We always took a vacation every year. That was fun. I played football, wrestled, and ran track. In church I played drums, led

jason

backstage {BE} exclusive

worship for youth, and sang solos all the time. Being a pastor's kid—I loved it growing up! I never hated it. There was no undue pressure. We could eat with the visiting musicians or evangelists, and we really liked these privileges. That usually surprises people!

Stupid questions:

What's the best thing about being a boy? We don't have to give birth.

The worst thing? Having to shave.

Favorite Charlie's Angel?
Not really into that.

Favorite CDs? Boyz II Men, Fred Hammond, Brian McKnight, worship stuff.

Favorite classes in school? Gym and lunch. Probably speech and debate, too. I always enjoyed being in front.

What's been hard about being famous? I don't really feel any different. One hard thing is being so busy. All the demands on your time and people calling you to be there. You don't own your own schedule. It's made for you. Sometimes on your days off it's nice to do whatever you want and be lazy.

Piercings? No.

Do you have a car? Yes, a 1987 Buick Park Avenue.

Who's the most popular Plus One member?
Can I pass on this one?

Who's the best dancer? Nathan.

Who's the most fun to hang out with? There are different things I enjoy about all the guys.

What do you value the most in a friendship? Trust.

What's your favorite Bible verse?
Chapter-wise it's Romans 8, but verse-wise it's John 15:16: "You did not choose me; I chose you to go and bear fruit." It's nothing I've done to be in this position.

What do you look for in women? Holiness—someone striving for godliness.

When did you become a Christian?
I was saved about a thousand times growing up in the church. But probably when I was seventeen, I really made a commitment to God—deciding that I really want to walk in His ways. I still made mistakes and didn't always prove my repentance by my deeds. But when God began to transform me was Halloween, 2000, when I met my pastor and stopped making decisions based on my feelings. He challenged me to memorize Scripture and introduced me to true Lordship and discipleship.

What or who inspired you to sing? Boyz II Men—Wanya's voice. I knew that I wanted to sing like that. I knew I wanted to sing and thought it'd probably be in church music ministry. I grew up listening to Steven Curtis Chapman and dc talk—straight pop.

What's your favorite food? Chicken.

What's your favorite TV show? SportsCenter.

What's your favorite hang out? The mall, anyplace with food, movies.

What's your most embarrassing moment? This past tour, when we were in Maryville, Indiana. We started the show in robes, singing a cappella, "It Is Well." Then came sound effects, and we ripped the robes off. I had on a button-down shirt, and I went to rip my robe open and my whole shirt opened. Then the dancing started, and I couldn't get my shirt buttoned.

What's your favorite season? I love them all, the different feelings in all. Summer and fall probably the best.

What's your favorite Plus One song? "God Is In This Place." I love the beat; the vibe is phat. I love the lyric, the Spanish guitar.

Siblings and Ages– Aaron 20, Curtis 15, Christy 14.

What's your favorite holiday? Christmas.

What is your favorite book? I'm not a huge reader; I probably should be.

What is your favorite place to shop? Diesel, Abercrombie & Fitch.

Who is your favorite actress/actor? Julia Roberts, Jim Carrey.

What is your favorite sport? Basketball.

What is your favorite thing to do in your spare time? Play b'ball, hang out, chill.

Who is your favorite team? Lakers.

Who is your favorite singer/artist? Brian McKnight, Michael English, Fred Hammond.

What is your favorite outfit that you own? Diesel jeans—I love them!

What is your favorite drink? Cherry Sprite.

What's your idea of the perfect date? Hanging out with a bunch of people, really getting to know the girl as a friend, and getting to know who she hangs around with.

Where do you go when you like to be alone? My car.

What is your favorite quote? A pastor from South Africa said, "The measure of a great leader is not how many people he leads, but how many people he serves."

What is your dream car? '64 Impala: baby blue, two doors, white leather interior, convertible.

What is your favorite cologne or perfume? Cool Water.

Who is your favorite Bible person? Paul or King David.

If you were not singing now, what would you want to be doing? I'd probably be at college pursuing the ministry.

jason

backstage {BE} exclusive

Lights! Camera! Action!

Plus One has filmed four music videos for songs from
The Promise: "Written On My Heart," "God Is In This
Place," "Last Flight Out," and "Here In My Heart."

Shooting the videos—was it like you thought it would be?

GABE: "Written"—That was awesome. You do a bunch of takes. I thought they'd be done really fast, but it took two full days. We spent a lot of time going over dancing. Making videos is a lot of rushing to wait. And when you finally film, it requires a lot of takes to get the right shot. For "Last Flight Out" we watched a video with twenty girls. Then we picked out the model we each wanted for the video. I just saw mine on a cover of *Lucky.* magazine!

JASON: The first video for "Written" was probably the most fun to make because we didn't know what to expect. All we knew was like, "Wow, here we are shooting a music video!!" They slowed down the track that we danced to, so when they played it back, it was really sharp. "Here In My Heart" was shot in Singapore. The location was amazing. It was actually a back lot of an old Chinese town. It was really cool. Oh, and I'm wearing a suit. Yeah, it's phat! We all had great clothes.

JEREMY: It wasn't like I thought it would be. I thought there was only a director, someone behind a camera, and the artist. That's definitely not the case. There are so many people involved! There are people doing lights, people messing with props, wardrobe, extras, and

18

anything else you can think of. It can become very tiring. But all of our videos have been fun to make and hopefully a lot more fun to watch!

NATE: It can be uncomfortable because you want to be cool, but you don't want to look like you're trying to be cool. A music video is supposed to make you look cool, but you don't want to look like you're trying too hard. If you look like you're having a good time, other people will see that, too. "God" was really fun because it was laid back. Plus, we shot it on the beach in California, and the water was freezing! "Here In My Heart" was awesome because we were all the way around the world in Asia. It was filmed by the director who shot my favorite Christian music video—"Consume Me" by dc talk.

NATHAN: For "Written" we didn't know what to expect. It was kind of like MTV's *Making the Video!* Shooting a music video is exciting, but it is also one of the most boring processes to go through. I sweat a lot, so most of the time during my takes there were about three or four people on the side wiping the sweat off of my body. I found that you have to learn to trust the director—that what he tells you is going to look right, even though it might not feel like it at the time. The best part about doing a video is getting new clothes.

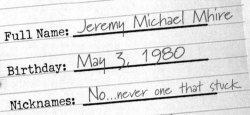

Full Name: _Jeremy Michael Mhire_

Birthday: _May 3, 1980_

Nicknames: _No...never one that stuck._

Born in Charlotte, NC—
went to H.S. in Springfield, MO

Jeremy is . . .

JASON: He likes to go against the grain. He's very outspoken.

GABE: He's very opinionated, very confident in what he does.

NATHAN: He's strong-willed. He's got his opinion down. Yet he's very cool at the same time. He's very sensitive to other people. He always tries to go for what's true in life. He's a good lyric writer.

NATE: Really opinionated.

HIMSELF: Musically, I think one of my best qualities is that I can hear parts. I can hear the song before it is mastered and mixed and know the direction to take the song. Personality-wise, I'm like Jason and have a strong will to succeed and excel. I can get competitive. I think I've been blessed with the ability to put my thoughts into words well.

Growing up:

Favorite memories: Probably playing with my dad. He has always taken the time to be there for us as a family. Both of my parents have always gone the extra mile to play with us and appreciate us. We had a half-acre behind the house, and we'd lay there and just look at the clouds. Or when I'd be playing football and basketball, they'd always be there. I am so grateful for that. Growing up as the oldest, I remember when my sister was born. I was three. Playing with her and fighting, those are good memories, too! When my brother was born, that was so cool. We got along so well. I was always singing in church. I could hear the parts. By the time I was seven or eight, I could harmonize by ear. Through seventh grade I was always involved in choir. It was always what I did, but it wasn't something I loved to do. I just did it. Sports were my love—basketball and football. I was really competitive. I wanted to be good. But in high school, I had a choir director who really encouraged me, and I got into All-State choir and had a great experience. I realized that was what I wanted to do.

jeremy

Stupid questions:

What's the best thing about being a boy?
Probably not having to go through childbirth.

The worst thing? Shaving everyday.

Favorite CDs? Radiohead, Fred Hammond, Harry Connick, Jr. (any one of his CDs), Coldplay.

Favorite classes in school? I'm right-brained, so I was good at English and history. My dad's a real history nut. I like *Jeopardy*. I'll knock it out. I love to go through history books and find out how we got to where we are now. I'm so not good at math and science.

What's been hard about being famous? The rigorous schedule. You're never in one place for any time. You can get lonely. You go to a show and there are thousands of people. Then on the bus, it's quiet; and it's just you. That can be tough. People are just pulling at you a lot of time. You have to be able to discern well, even with people you think are your friends. You have to watch people's motives.

Do you have a car? A pick-up truck, but it's back home.

Who's the most popular Plus One member? Probably with our fan base, Nate.

Who's the best dancer? Probably myself or Nathan.

Who's the most fun to hang out with? Depends on what mood I'm in.

What do you value the most in a friendship? Trust and sincerity.

What's your favorite Bible verse? Proverbs 18:12.

When did you become a Christian? I was raised in a non-denominational church knowing every Sunday I had to go to church. I didn't really understand. It wasn't until I tried to abandon my faith, probably when I got in high school, when you have so many doubts about God and your faith. Not until I let go of that did I realize how much God really had His hand on my life. I see now how everything that has happened has come together to make me what I am now, to bring me here into God's perfect will.

Where do you go when you like to be alone? Before the group, I lived in Springfield, Missouri. I went to the football field and sat in the stands. I do that now, too. I think in the shower a lot, also.

What do you look for in women? A girl that doesn't have "round heels." Meaning, I don't want a partner who's going to fall over backwards anytime there's a dispute. If you're wrong, she's going to tell you. She'll stand firm. Someone who's caring, loving, and who loves God.

Piercings? Yes. Eyebrow, two in left ear, and the top cartilage.

What or who inspired you to sing? My parents.

What's your favorite food? Steak.

What's your favorite TV show? *Whose Line Is It Anyway*? It used to be *Mystery Science Theater*. We'd mute the sound and make up our own dialogue.

What's your favorite hang out? Coffee places and the magazine section of Barnes & Noble.

What's your most embarrassing moment? In first grade I decided to urinate on the playground to be funny and stupid. Everyone was laughing, but the teacher started flying towards me. Someone saw me and called the school, and they had to tell my parents. I got in trouble.

What's your favorite season? Spring.

What's your favorite Plus One song? "Last Flight Out."

Siblings and Ages–Joshua 9, Rachel 18.

What's your favorite holiday? Christmas.

Who is your favorite team? Kansas Jayhawks—KU.

What is your favorite book? *The Prayer of Jabez.*

Who is your favorite cartoon character? Scooby Doo.

What is your favorite place to shop? New York at Diesel, H&M.

Who is your favorite actress/actor? Charlize Theron, Al Pacino.

What is your favorite sport? Football, basketball.

What is your favorite thing to do in your spare time? Hang with girlfriend, shop, keep up with Jayhawks, or work out.

Who is your favorite singer/artist? Harry Connick, Jr.

What is your favorite outfit that you own? Probably our tour outfits.

What is your favorite drink? Kiwi Strawberry, Coke, water.

Favorite boy and girl names? Girl—Adria, boy—Preston.

What's your idea of the perfect date? Sushi, coffee, and a great movie.

What is your favorite quote? Whenever I don't feel like going to work, I remember what David (Foster) said to us, "Work hard while you're young. Play hard when you're an adult. If you play when you're young, you'll work hard when you're an adult."

What is your dream car? Classic cars, a roadster, old-school Mercedes.

What is your favorite cologne or perfume? Cologne: Emporio Armani. Diesel perfume.

Who is your favorite Bible person? David.

If you were not singing now, what would you want to be doing? Acting.

jeremy

It's interesting to see fans react differently in different cities. I enjoy talking in the show. It gives the fans a chance to see who we are and tell them about our message more in-depth. —Jason

hit the road

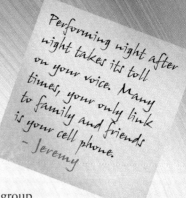

Performing night after night takes its toll on your voice. Many times, your only link to family and friends is your cell phone.
– Jeremy

What's your favorite part about touring and doing concerts?

JASON: Performing live, making people smile, and having a good time. Seeing people respond to what we say. I like being in a group that people can show to their friends.

GABE: Being on stage. That's just one of the coolest feelings. You feel so loved. The traveling is hard. It gets tiring, but you get to see so many different people and states. It's hard when you go some place and you're tired, but you're meeting people for the first time. You still have to give that good first impression.

JEREMY: Being on stage. Sometimes it's easy to get frustrated because you sit around a lot. Then you get to get on stage and feel the music and relate to the audience.

NATHAN: Food. Can you tell I love food? Being on stage. It's a lot of work and waiting. My favorite part is when they announce us, and the crowd goes crazy—that first couple of minutes.

NATE: Traveling. Negative: living out of a suitcase. Great, though, when you're young. I like performing. I'm doing exactly what I love to do: singing.

I love touring, but there are days when I get really homesick. Then when I'm home I want to be touring. Seems like you always want what you can't have!

— Nathan

What do you do on the bus or plane to pass time?

NATHAN: On the plane I sleep. That's an art that I've developed. On the bus, I bring my equipment for great demos. I write constantly.

NATE: On the plane I listen to music. I'm not a reader, but every now and then I will read a good book. I listen to music a lot. On the bus, we'll stay up real late watching movies or playing PlayStation.

JEREMY: Watch DVDs or listen to music. I write a lot; I'm really into writing. I really like to document stuff. I don't always remember moments, but I remember what I journal.

JASON: Listen to music, read, write, watch movies, TV.

GABE: Listen to CDs or play guitar. I love that. Also writing music or watching DVDs on the bus.

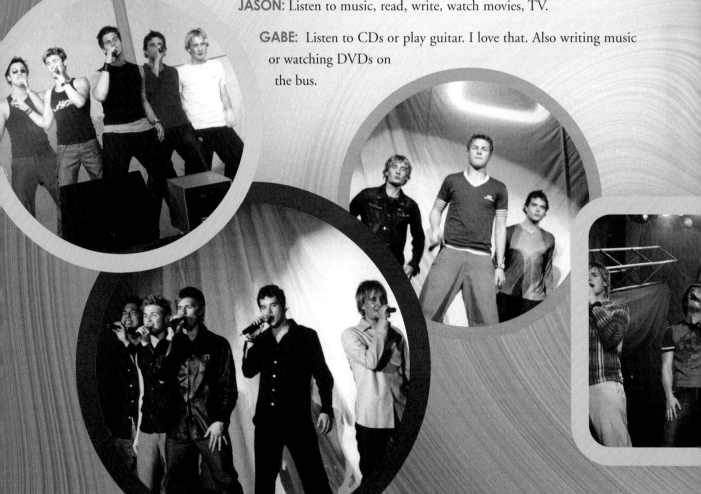

backstage {BE} exclusive

Do you pick out your own clothes for performing?

NATHAN: Yeah. Some shows we'll have a stylist that will buy clothes for us. And then we'll pick out what we want. I'd like to see us have more time and control over that, but that takes time and money. We have a lot of freedom to express ourselves.

NATE: There's never been a time we had to wear something we didn't want to wear. For the tour we have four outfits that we trade off each night.

What is the most meaningful part for you of being a performer?

NATHAN: Connecting with someone and changing how they feel about their day. Not just musically, but with the message of hope and really experiencing God. Even in mainstream events that can happen, if they can see that we're real and not flaky or judgmental.

NATE: While I'm out on stage, I'm performing for an audience of One. It really causes you to give one hundred ten percent. It's good to have a real spiritual focus, but also to just have fun, too. It doesn't have to be all serious when you're a Christian.

JEREMY: I'd say relating to the audience. My dad has tried to instill in me to always be genuine or sincere, whether on or off stage. Another thing is just getting the response from the audience. I think it's the best feeling that what you're doing—no matter what you're doing—is doing good for people. And to know that God is blessing your effort.

GABE: Seeing the impact we have on people's lives is amazing. We get letters all the time from people who have changed their lives because of a song we sang. It's an amazing thing.

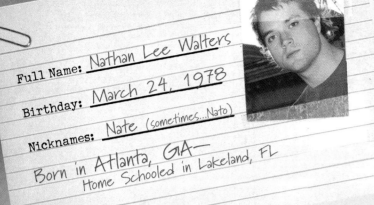

Full Name: Nathan Lee Walters

Birthday: March 24, 1978

Nicknames: Nate (sometimes...Nato)

Born in Atlanta, GA—
Home Schooled in Lakeland, FL

Nathan is...

JASON: A nice guy, very ambitious.

GABE: The most sincere guy in the group. The opposite of selfish. He's always defending others, taking a look at the other side. He's one of the nicest guys I've ever met, and he likes to suck in his cheekbones on every photo shoot.

JEREMY: He sings the high end with a really sweet tone. He's a great songwriter, one of the most developed. He has the most genuine heart for people. He really cares about people and their feelings. In a conversation, you can tell he's a great listener.

NATE: An all-around good guy. He's very kind and brings a lot of peace to situations. A people person.

HIMSELF: Someone who is open with people. Maybe I talk about too many things that are personal. I care about what other people think about, value their feelings, and make sure they're comfortable. I like to have fun but also be responsible. I'm a big prankster. I pull jokes on people all the time.

Growing up:

When I was five, six, or seven, I lived on Martha Avenue in Lakeland, Florida. That was the first street name I remember. I got my first dog and my first dog bite. I dug a big hole for my pet turtle. Also, I got a scar on my leg that looks like an index finger pointing upward. I played a lot with my brother. I started playing piano a lot in that house. First time someone stole my bike was there. We used to go to Joker Stadium for Tigers baseball spring training and would get autographs. I was home-schooled growing up, so we did a lot of stuff together. For nine years it was just my brother and I, and our family would go to Washington, D.C., or St. Augustine beach. Then my mom had four little girls. They are four to eleven now. We kind of became two different families, in a way. The family was still close, but we all started going in different directions.

Me and Ivan

nathan

Stupid questions:

What's the best thing about being a boy? Girls. And the fact that you can just wake up in the morning, brush your teeth, and go out and not worry about what you look like. We don't have to prepare as much. I love being a guy.

The worst thing? There might be some times guys have to be responsible. Also, if you're speeding and you get pulled over, you're more likely to get a ticket. Girls can get away with stuff like that better.

Favorite Charlie's Angel? Old, Jacquelyn Smith. New, Cameron Diaz.

Piercings? No. Was thinking about it—my nose. But I do like my nose. It's the only thing I really like on my face. I probably won't get a tattoo.

Favorite CDs? *The Promise*, of course! I was a big Michael W. Smith fan growing up—*Go West Young Man* brings out the best emotions and feelings. That CD made me want to be a songwriter. Brian McKnight's *Anytime*.

Who is your favorite singer/artist? Brian McKnight.

Favorite classes in school? Math—liked it a lot. It was easy; it made sense. I use a lot of math now in sequencing music. I really liked English, too. I liked conjugating. That was fun. Also, science. I liked mixing chemicals. And music, too.

Do you have a car? No, I sold it year and a half ago when we moved to California. But I haven't needed one since.

What's been hard about being famous? Nothing hard, but you get so busy. There's more stuff you have to do. We have to do all kinds of promotional things that take up so much time. To be on-call all the time. Your schedule is not your own. But I'm really happy all the time.

Who's the most popular Plus One member? It changes. Nate or Jason get the most screams; probably Nate because he's nice and cute. And he's got the girl-catcher voice.

Who's the best dancer? Everybody says it's me.

Who's the most fun to hang out with? It changes. We're all really good friends. Gabe and I hang out a lot. And we're sharing equipment.

What do you look for in women? Friendship first and someone who is not lazy, but very determined to succeed, really going after it. Going for the next thing. A good sense of style is nice to have. I really need someone in my life who understands my music and who appreciates what I do. Maybe someone who can write or someone who knows how to relate to other people, too.

What do you value the most in a friendship? Honesty—about themselves and you.

What's your favorite Bible verse? Once, I memorized the whole book of James. I really like Chapter 3. It talks about the tongue and makes me watch what I say, whether I'm joking or complaining.

When did you become a Christian? I was seven.

What or who inspired you to sing? Michael W. Smith.

What's your favorite food? Italian food, Chinese Chicken Salad. I'm getting into that. Or a Grilled Chicken Caesar Salad at O'Charleys or TGIFriday's.

What's your favorite TV show? Don't watch a lot.

What's your favorite hang out? My studio.

What's your most embarrassing moment? On stage once I was getting all excited and running around. I had a snap-up shirt, and Nate's mic ripped my shirt all the way open while I was dancing around. I had to try and snap it up before we started a dance move.

What's your favorite season? Fall.

What's your favorite Plus One song? "Soul Tattoo" and "Last Flight Out."

Siblings and Ages? Ivan 20, Lauren 11, Kathryn 9, Kiersten 5, Jacquelyn 4.

What's your favorite holiday? It's not Easter. I have bad memories of wearing a tie and suit as a kid. Christmas.

What is your favorite place to shop? Diesel.

What's your idea of the perfect date? Doing something creative and productive during the day. Maybe going to the beach.

What is your favorite sport? Soccer, baseball.

Who is your favorite team? Atlanta Braves.

What is your favorite outfit that you own? Jeans from Diesel. They're actually girl jeans extra-big. They flair out at the bottom.

What is your favorite book? *Just Like Jesus* by Max Lucado.

Who is your favorite actress/actor? Sandra Bullock, Harrison Ford.

What is your favorite drink? Sprite or 7-Up mixed with lemonade or Fling Tea at Cooker.

What is your favorite thing to do in your spare time? Studio stuff.

Where do you go when you like to be alone? My studio with headphones on, or I'll go drive around.

What is your favorite quote? "Remember that no one looks out for you better than yourself."

What is your dream car? Black Mercedes.

What is your favorite cologne or perfume? Cologne: Acqua di Gio' by Giorgio Armani. Perfume: Happy by Clinique.

Who is your favorite Bible person and why? John. He got the Revelation.

nathan

It's not what you might think...

What are the biggest misconceptions about being in Plus One?

NATHAN: That we're rich. We're not. We have sold a lot of albums, but we're not. To get ourselves out there, the label put a lot of money into us. Sometimes people think we're Christians, but that we're not really living it. We are loving God with all our hearts. We're pursuing Him. Some Christians thought we weren't Christians when we sang for the Democratic National Convention or were on *Days of Our Lives*. They don't understand why we're doing those things.

GABE: People think we're just put together and we'll end up doing this for two or three years and then do something else. God truly hand-picked each member of this group, and we'll be here for a while to minister. People don't see the real impact we're having.

NATE: That we're rich. My siblings get asked if we have a lot of money. I used to think that you'd be a millionaire when you make a record. Some people think that since we're young and do this music, we lack depth. Until they meet us or see our concert, they're making a judgment. Some people think that we're just Christian guys who are trying to make it big in the mainstream and just using Christian music. Even if we get more successful, we're not going to change our message.

JEREMY: That Plus One is a marketing ploy. People are going to think what they're going to think. We have to make sure that our motives are pure. People will see it more in our actions than anything I ever say in an interview. Friends think I'm rich now. It's cool that a lot of stuff is paid for. But cash in my pocket—no.

JASON: That we're rich—that we have money. Lord knows we don't have money. People write us off as just another boy band that doesn't have much to say. If people can get past the fact that we're young guys, they see that we really have some good things to say. I want to be a nineteen-year-old man who loves God, to really show other young men that it's possible to live a life of holiness and purity before God.

Full Name: Nathan David Forest Cole

Birthday: May 19, 1981

Nicknames: Nate or Nate Dog

Born in Houston, TX— went to H.S. in Sacramento, CA

Nate is . . .

JASON: The cute one—just a nice guy.

GABE: There's a very innocent thing about him, but also very gullible. I tell him stories all the time, and he believes them. He's a good listener and a good speaker at the same time.

JEREMY: Musically, he's a strong lead vocal and good at coming up with ad-libs and melodies. He's also a good writer. I think he's really wise. You can see the wisdom God has given him to discern right from wrong.

NATHAN: He's always been a really good guy. Everybody likes him. He has a mischievous side, too. Nothing bad, but something fun.

HIMSELF: Considerate.

Growing up:

I have a lot of high school memories. Proms, Homecoming, playing sports. Lots of memories of bus rides with the guys. I played basketball, golf, football, and baseball, even though I wasn't necessarily a jock. I grew up in California, then spent four years in Omaha, Nebraska, from fourth grade through eighth grade. But most memories are in California. All my memories at home were totally cool. That made it hard to move away, because I got along so well with everyone. My sister and I hated each other growing up. But when we started high school, all of the sudden we were like, "We're so stupid. Why are we fighting?" My parents are like my friends. I miss the normal stuff like going out to dinner together, cracking up together, laughing, or

nate

nate

going to youth group. I'm learning guitar from Gabe. He's really talented.

Stupid questions:

What's the best thing about being a boy? Girls. I really like being a guy.

The worst thing? It seems like there's more responsibility if you're a guy.

Favorite Charlie's Angel? I don't have one.

Favorite CDs? New Boyz II Men album. One of my all-time favorites is dc talk's *Jesus Freak*—love that album. Fred Hammond's *Spirit of David* is my favorite worship album.

Favorite classes in school? I wasn't much of a student. I didn't enjoy math. I was terrible. I hated it so much. I enjoy biology and that stuff, like experiments and dissecting things. That was fun.

What's been hard about being famous? Your life becomes more public. I'll get e-mails asking me if I'm dating certain people. Our fans talk about that stuff. They care if you have a girlfriend. Why in the world do I have to tell anybody about that? Everything is watched. You have to be more careful.

Piercings? No. I've been tempted to. But my grandpa and parents wouldn't be very excited. My grandparents will think I've lost it. They want me to be clean-cut.

Do you have a car? Honda Civic Silver, '97. Nothing special. I like it.

Who's the most popular Plus One member? I don't know.

Who's the best dancer? Nathan. He can do some scary Michael Jackson impressions.

Who's the most fun to hang out with? Gabe. We're real close.

What do you value the most in a friendship? Trust. I can't stand people who lie.

What's your favorite Bible verse? Proverbs 3:5-6.

When did you become a Christian? I was four when I prayed with my mom after hearing the story of Jonah and the whale. My sophomore year in high school is when I realized that it's something I have to do on my own.

What's your most embarrassing moment? One time we were going to run out on stage. I was the first one, and there were these steps. I jumped up onto the steps, and they were on rollers. They flew out from under me, and everybody saw me fall onto stage.

What do you look for in women? Honesty. That's the main thing. Physical things are the least important, as I get older. But at the same time, you're not going to go after someone you're not attracted to. She has to be a Christian. Also, someone who's fun and not too serious.

What or who inspired you to sing? My mom. I sang in children's choir when I was really young. I listened to Steven Curtis Chapman all the time. I'd always sing along. One day she bought me a track for "No Better Place" and said, "I think you should sing this song in church." *There's no way,* I thought. I was terrified. I didn't even want to sing it in my house by myself. My mom kept encouraging me and praying for me. From then on, I kept singing. My mom's dad was a singer/songwriter—Ira Stanphill. He wrote "I Know Who Holds Tomorrow." Leann Rimes recorded that. There's a little bit of that in me.

What's your favorite TV show? *Fresh Prince of Bel Air.*

What's your favorite Plus One song? "Last Flight Out." I really like the vibe of it. Or "God Is In This Place." It really invites God into the place during the concert.

What's your favorite season? Spring.

Siblings and Ages– Laine 17, Travis 16.

What's your favorite holiday? Christmas.

What is your favorite book? *Run Baby Run* by Nicky Cruz. He's the *Cross & The Switchblade* guy.

What is your favorite place to shop? In New York at a place called H&M. Really cool stuff for really good prices.

Who is your favorite cartoon character? Alvin from the Chipmunks.

What is your favorite sport? Basketball.

Who is your favorite team? Kings.

What's your favorite food? Taco Bell—fast food.

What is your favorite drink? Water.

What is your favorite thing to do in your spare time? Write songs for the new album now or just hang out time to do nothing. A movie, maybe.

Who is your favorite actress/actor? Julia Roberts, Will Smith.

Who is your favorite singer/artist? Wanya from Boyz II Men.

What is your favorite outfit that you own? Sometimes I'll wear a dressy look, but I like wearing vintage t-shirts with jeans that are more fitted—even cowboy shirts!

Favorite girl name? Kendall.

What's your idea of the perfect date? It depends on the person, but something to do would be to go somewhere really nice for dinner where you dress up. Then we'd change clothes and be more casual, then find a lookout spot on a mountain. Just watching the stars and having a good conversation about life.

Where do you go when you like to be alone? I'll go driving sometimes and end up at a grocery store looking at magazines.

What is your dream car? I'd like to own a Hummer.

What is your favorite cologne or perfume? A new kind I really like is called Angel for Men.

HERE IN MY heart

How would you describe your relationship with God?

NATHAN: Right now, things are good. There was a time when I moved away. I grew up in the church and really tried to be a good Christian. But the time came when I began questioning some things and started running with people who twisted some things. Then I came to the understanding that my parents were actually right, and that my relationship with God needs to be real. I want a three-dimensional relationship where I am in Him, and He is in me. I'm never satisfied with my relationship with God. I want more. I'm on a journey of trying to get closer. You don't have joy all the time. If you're a Christian, you're going to have peace. You're not going to be happy all the time. You might even feel left out sometimes. But He can be your best friend or helper. You've got peace, security, and eternal life.

NATE: It's constantly changing, growing. I'm questioning a lot trying to know the heart of God and really understand how He would handle situations and how He would treat people. It has to be a one-on-one relationship, just hanging out with him. It's really all about prayer and reading the Bible. I have to make an effort. It just can't be a complement to my life. Accountability is vital in a relationship with God. It's easier if you have someone pushing you in the right direction. Being a Christian, you don't have to worry about life. Lots of people are worriers. For those who love God, one of the benefits is knowing He works all things for our good. God is always there. You're never alone. We're all 'plus One.'

JEREMY: I'd say over the past year and a half, I've really come to understand and feel God's touch on my life. It's a daily, constant renewing of a relationship—like with anyone. I realize a lot now that the effort for me to maintain my relationship with God has to be sincere and genuine to really get somewhere. As far as feeling pressure to be perfect, that's pressure that you put on yourself. You're never going to be able to live up to anyone's standards. You can only be guided by the Holy Spirit. I can't base my convictions on what other people think. If I am doing this to show everybody I'm a perfect Christian, I'll never be able to do that. God is where I find my happiness and strength.

JASON: It's strong, growing, becoming deeper. God is really beginning to pull me in. I'm really seeking Him to find out what His heart is for me personally to walk and fulfill my destiny. I'm reading and learning so much from the Word. I don't have it all together. I'm not perfect. I'm learning and growing. Paul said in the New Testament, "Not that I have already obtained all this or have already been made perfect, but I press on to take hold of that for which Christ Jesus took hold of me." I like it when young people ask me questions and look up to me. I want them to see that I'm striving. We're ready to raise the standard. Too many artists have fallen. I'm not here to do that. God is looking for people who are going to count the cost and be obedient.

GABE: It's like a friendship—more of a closer friend. Sometimes I'll just pray and tell Him what I'm thinking, what my thoughts were that day. I know He's listening. God is just a cool friend that sticks closer than a brother. Friends come and go, but He'll never leave. Sometimes I get the feeling that people are waiting for us to do something wrong, so they can point their fingers at us. It gets hard sometimes. Sometimes you just don't want to care, 'cause they shouldn't be looking at me but at God. But we do have to watch what we do.

plus
ONE

Full Name: Gabriel Corbitt Combs

Birthday: Dec 11, 1979

Nicknames: Family calls me, Dabsky
from my nephew who couldn't say my name.
He said Dab—and it turned into Dabsky.

Born in Salem, OR—
went to H.S. in Pittsburgh, CA

Gabe is . . .

JASON: A funny guy—goofy funny.

NATE: A totally fun guy, but he's usually quiet if you don't know him. He has a very original kind of humor. He doesn't follow the crowd. He likes to be different with his music and clothes.

JEREMY: Musically, he's one of the most talented instrumentally in the group. He can play anything and everything very well. You'd think from first impressions that he's shy, but he's the comic relief of the group. He's like a walking cartoon. He's so funny, almost quirky. He's also a real good peacemaker. He brings reason when there's dispute.

NATHAN: He's really goofy. I'm always laughing at him. Not at what he says, but how he says it. He's good at impressions of people.

HIMSELF: He's the goofiest one in the group. He likes to joke around. He's probably a pretty good listener. He likes to listen to problems and give solutions.

Growing up:

I have two older brothers four and eight years apart. We had a lot of fun. Our parents left us alone a lot, and we'd go play music down at my dad's church. We'd fight a lot when we were younger. A lot of people think being a preacher's kid is bad, but it was really cool being so involved in the church, especially in the music areas and drama. It really prepared me for being in front of crowds and performing. It's training you can't get anywhere else. I started learning different instruments at eleven years old and began playing drums in the Sunday morning service. I'd come home and try to figure out worship songs on the piano. My mom encouraged me a lot. And in junior high I would figure songs out by ear on the piano just from being in church and developing an ear for music. Now I play guitar, drums, bass, and piano. I was usually in band, played piano. I couldn't read music, but they'd play the song a couple of times and I'd figure it out. Also drama, school choir, and youth choir. My school was in the same region as Nate's, and we had competition one year together. That was the first time I saw him. He was being

gabe

really loud and confident. He got one of the solos in the big group choir.

Stupid questions:

What's the best thing about being a boy? You get to grow facial hair.

The worst thing? Can't think of anything.

Favorite Charlie's Angel? New, Cameron Diaz, but I love Drew Barrymore's personality.

Favorite CDs? Radiohead's *Kid A*, dc talk's *Jesus Freak*, Beatles' *1* hits, and the new Boyz II Men album.

Piercings? I recently pierced the hard cartilage of my ear on the front. I had both ears and my nose pierced. I think I'm going through a stage. But I just kept one. I thought about the impression on parents and kids, even though piercing doesn't change who I am.

Favorite classes in school? P.E.

Worst? Math, hated it. I was so bad in math. I don't know how I passed. I loved music class. One year I had a great teacher and learned a lot of music theory.

What's been hard about being famous? You meet new people all the time for the first time. You have to be nice to them, even if you're tired or mad. It's not their fault that they caught you on a bad day. Or maybe just having people looking at you all the time.

Do you have a car? I'm getting one. A new Volkswagen Beetle, a black one with CD changer. I'm just waiting on the bank right now.

Who's the most popular PLUS ONE member? Hard to say. It's weird. We'll go to different areas, and one person will be and then another. Closer to L.A., everyone loved Jeremy. In San Jose, it was me. Or some other place, Nathan. Overall Nate or Jason—they're tied.

Who's the best dancer? Nathan. No—me. No—Nathan. He's totally Michael Jackson. Even when he's fooling around, he's so good.

Who's the most fun to hang out with? I dunno. Besides me? Probably me. I'm the most easy going and carefree. I'm out to have fun.

What do you value the most in a friendship? Honesty. Without that, you really don't have a true friendship.

What's your favorite Bible verse? Romans Chapter 12—Paul speaking about presenting our body as a living and holy sacrifice. It has so much good information in it.

What do you look for in women? Someone who likes to have fun, although I'm not sure if that's good for me. I'd like to meet a girl who knows what she wants.

When did you become a Christian? In junior high and high school, I started to realize it for myself—after growing up in the church.

What or who inspired you to sing? Probably my brothers. They had really good voices. They were good writers, too. I thought it was really cool.

What's your favorite food? Taco Bell Nacho Grande.

What's your favorite TV show? VH1's *Behind the Music.* I could watch that for days: Seeing bands like Def Leppard or Metallica and what has happened to them.

What's your most embarrassing moment? I was on stage, and I was really getting into it in a mall packed out with three thousand kids really close to the stage. I threw my hand out to the audience, and my mic fell out of my hand and hit a girl straight on the head. I just went down and grabbed the mic and kept singing. From then on, she was really mad at me. But we made up afterwards.

What's your favorite season? Fall—wearing heavy clothes.

What's your favorite Plus One song? "Last Flight Out." I can listen to that over and over.

Siblings and ages? Josh 24, Tim 28.

What's your favorite holiday? Christmas.

What is your favorite book? dc talk's *Jesus Freaks*—very cool.

Who is your favorite cartoon character? Droopy.

What is your favorite place to shop? Diesel.

Who is your favorite actress/actor? Angelina Jolie, Jim Carrey.

What is your favorite sport? Basketball.

What is your favorite thing to do in your spare time? Shop, go to movies, and write music.

Who is your favorite team? L.A. Lakers.

Who is your favorite singer/artist? Radiohead.

What is your favorite outfit that you own? My style changes every day. Some days it's really weird. There's not really a favorite.

What is your favorite drink? Strawberry banana smoothie.

What's your idea of the perfect date? Something that's not too traditional. Something that's not even considered a date. Maybe like going to the beach and talking, hanging out all day and night. Maybe going to a different city or state.

Where do you go when you like to be alone? Take a walk somewhere like across the street to Kroger to read magazines.

What is your dream car? I'll change tomorrow, but how about a Viper?

What is your favorite cologne or perfume? Cologne, Diesel. Acqua di Gio'.

Who is your favorite Bible person and why? Paul. He wrote half the New Testament.

If you were not singing now, what would you want to be doing? Writing and producing in the industry somehow.

gabe

Facing the FUTURE

What do you hope to accomplish in the next five years, ten years—personally and with the group?

GABE: I'd like to have a house, be settled down, and have a family or something. I hope to start my own record label. I want to be involved in producing and starting other groups. We all came to the reality that Plus One isn't going to be around forever, so we are doing what we can to prepare for the future.

JASON: I'd like to see our albums sell a lot. But whether we do or not, I want to accomplish what God has for us. I'd like to develop other areas of my life—writing a book, developing other kinds of relationships, becoming a full-statured man of God. The biggest thing that will determine our path as Plus One is how focused we stay on the goal— on why we are here, and who we're doing this for. I pray that God would accomplish everything He wants to do with Plus One and not be hindered by our own selfish ambitions and desires. I hope we'll always do it for His glory.

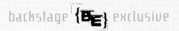

JEREMY: I hope we can keep getting better and excelling as a band and that our songwriting abilities will get better. Just to have God use us as He will. Personally, I want to go to the Eiffel Tower. I want to see the world a lot more. I plan to continue writing music, hopefully get into producing, maybe try to act, maybe get into fashion, designing, and perhaps photography. I might try a solo career in a different genre of music. Oh yeah, I also plan to grow my hair long, try to stay fit, get married, and have kids—but all that might be way down the line.

NATHAN: I'd like to hopefully develop both my writing and my producing side. In ten years, I need to be married, living away from these guys. Hopefully in the next year! I'd like to write, produce, and travel on the weekends with my wife.

NATE: I hope we can continue really staying true. I hope that we don't change as individuals. I hope we can continue moving into the mainstream, affecting the culture, really making a difference—like modern-day Bible characters! I hope to continue writing music. I feel like I'd like to do a solo project. We're all continuing our pursuit of excellence in all aspects of our ministry.

fear not

Do you have any particular insecurity that you'd like to share?

JASON: I have struggled with finding my identity in the past as a person, but I've really come to find it in my Christ Jesus—finding who I am and serving Him.

GABE: Sometimes I'm insecure about my voice. When I was trying out for the group, I was thinking, "What if they don't like my voice?"

JEREMY: One of my insecurities has been thinking, "Is my voice really that good after all?" Being in the music industry you realize you're not the best singer in the world. There are tons of people who can sing better than you. I really have found my place in the group where I know what I can or can't do vocally. I've got more of a handle on it now.

NATE: I used to be insecure around my guy friends, because to a lot of guys, boy bands are made fun of. I want them to think it's cool what I'm doing. But with the success that we've had, now they think my group's cool.

NATHAN: I've been insecure about my cheeks. Sometimes I wish I were more cut, more chiseled. When I was younger, I would suck in my cheeks for fun. Now I do it out of habit. The guys make fun of me for that. I used to be really insecure about communicating with people, especially people in authority, worrying about saying the wrong thing.

My Friend

What would you like to say to your fans?

GABE: A lot of people are trying to do stuff that they're not good at—trying to believe they are something that they aren't. Be yourself, and go do what you're good at. Really hone in on your skills.

JASON: That Plus One has a hope and faith in Jesus Christ. We want to challenge young people: pursue your destiny and your purpose in life. He created you to do good work and has a plan for your life, so you should begin to seek that out. But most importantly, receive Jesus as Lord of your life if you haven't yet.

JEREMY: Thank you. Whenever people or your family lets you down, there's always going to be God there in the end.

NATE: People are constantly asking us how to get into the music business. I'd like to say that instead of seeking out all your own desires, ask God what He wants for your life. That's what you'll be the happiest doing—and the most fulfilled. Dream big.

NATHAN: We don't want to come across preachy. We want to make sure we show God's love. We've found in our lives that when we trust God and try to experience Him, our lives are a lot better. We're normal guys. Sometimes we mess up, but our main focus is on God.

plus ONE Just the facts

THE PROMISE:

RELEASED May 2000 on 143 Records/ Atlantic Records.

DEBUTED AT #1 on the SoundScan Christian music chart and #76 on the *Billboard* 200.

CERTIFIED GOLD (selling 500,000 albums) within ten months of its release.

PLUS ONE was the Best-Selling Artist of the Christian market in 2000.

AWARDS & ACCOLADES:

2001 – DOVE AWARD for New Artist of the Year.

2001 – DOVE AWARD NOMINATIONS:

- Group of the Year.
- Pop/Contemporary Album of the Year for *The Promise*.
- Pop/Contemporary Recorded Song – "Written On My Heart."
- Song of the Year – "Written On My Heart."

SOUNDTRACK CONTRIBUTIONS:

"WITH ALL YOUR HEART" appeared on Atlantic Records' *Pokémon 2000: The Power of One* soundtrack.

"I NEED A MIRACLE" appeared on the soundtrack for *Left Behind: The Movie*.

RADIO SUCCESS:

"WRITTEN ON MY HEART" – #1 AC for three weeks, **#1 CHR** for seven weeks.

"GOD IS IN THIS PLACE" – #1 AC for one week.

"THE PROMISE" – #1 AC for two weeks.

"MY LIFE" – #1 CHR for one week.

CHRISTIAN RADIO FORMATS:

AC - Adult Contemporary, CHR - Contemporary Hits

VIDEO SUCCESS:

"WRITTEN ON MY HEART" scored #1 most-requested status on the Disney Channel.

MAGAZINE COVER STORIES:

CCM Magazine, Release, Brio, Campus Life, and *GMA Today*

TV APPEARANCES:

Disney, Nickelodeon, ABC, NBC, CBS, BBC, TNN, and WGN—including appearances on *Days of Our Lives* and *Touched By An Angel*.

CONTACT INFORMATION:

LABEL: 143 Records/Atlantic Records

MANAGEMENT: Mitchell Artist Management

BOOKING: William Morris Agency

www.plusoneonline.com